Key Notes
The History of
The Lerwick Orchestra

Key Notes
The History of
The Lerwick Orchestra

by

Susan Cooper

Susan Cooper.

The Shetland Times Ltd.,
Lerwick.
1996

Cover design by the Stafford Partnership, Shetland.

ISBN 1 898852 13 8

British Library Cataloguing-in-Publication Data
A catalogue record for this book is available from the British Library.

Printed and published by The Shetland Times Ltd.,
Prince Alfred Street, Lerwick, Shetland, ZE1 0EP.

Contents

Foreword VI

Introduction VII

Chapter One — The Early Years 1

Chapter Two — Gilbert and Sullivan Operas 16

Chapter Three — A. R. M. Mathewson 20

Chapter Four — Post War Conductors 29

Chapter Five — The Sixties and Seventies 39

Chapter Six — Dr T. M. Y. Manson and the Present Day 46

Chapter Seven — Members' Music 51

Bibliography 54

Illustrations 55

Foreword

Having spent much time over a long period as a playing member and office-bearer of a long standing body of amateur musicians, the Lerwick Orchestral Society, it gives me the greatest pleasure to write the foreword to a new publication about that society.

The book is due to the initiative and work of a member of the society who plays the clarinet and is my immediate successor as secretary.

I hope the society will continue to contribute to the musical life of Lerwick.

T. M. Y. Manson
Viewforth Eventide Home, 1995

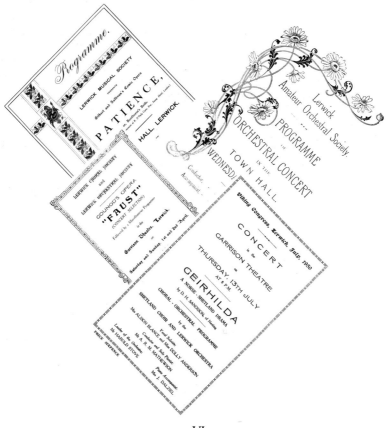

Introduction

When I took over the job as Secretary to the Lerwick Orchestra from Dr. T.M.Y. Manson it became very clear to me that I had acquired a vast amount of material about the group going back over a long period of time.

Dr. Manson's connection with *The Shetland News* and his meticulous note-taking inspired me to find out more about the players and what they did for a living.

My research would have been difficult without the help of many people. Thanks go to Miss Enid Belshaw, Mike Blyth, Mr G. I. de Mercado, Hilary Harmer, Mrs Hurlock, Pryde Johnson, Douglas Johnstone, Mr & Mrs Billy Kay, Mrs Jessie Leask, Captain M. Linklater, Bertha Martin, Miss Helen Morris, Miss Nessie Robertson, Mr Frank Scott, Magnus Shearer, John Shepherd, Douglas and Meg Smith, Pam Smith, Mr Magnus Stove, Mrs Jean Thomason, Mr J. Wishart, Mrs Barbara Sandison, the Registrar, and Douglas Garden, with the staff at the Library who have been so helpful putting on the microfilm.

Mr Ian Tait of the Shetland Museum has spent a considerable amount of time looking out photographs and the Archives staff, especially Brian Smith, have given encouragement and technical advice at all stages of the project, along with Mr John Graham. The book would have not been possible without this help, thank you.

Last but not least Dr. Manson and his infallible memory. This is a tribute to his years of service to the orchestra.

Susan Cooper 1996

The Early Years

It is the evening of 27th April, 1904. In the Lerwick Town Hall Thomas Manson's baton comes down to open Wagner's grand march, *Tannhäuser*. Rich harmonies and lovely melodies were beautifully brought out by the full orchestra. The audience were given a foretaste of the good things in store for them. Underway is the first concert given by the Lerwick Amateur Orchestral Society. What of music in Shetland before then?

There is some thought that musical influences reached Shetland from Norway before 1469. Undoubtedly origins are more on the Scandinavian side of the water than Scotland. The connections with the Hardanger fiddle confirm that.

Edmondston said in 1809: "One in ten peasantry could play the violin." In 1814 Sir Walter Scott, on a visit to Shetland, made the acquaintance of two maiden ladies by the name of Campbell who kept a small boarding school. Scott sent them a handsome pianoforte, so it is said, as he was so interested in their efforts to maintain a position of independence. They were the Misses Dorothea and Eliza Campbell. The piano was sold to Hosea Hoseason in Yell for his daughter.

Great strides were made in 1827 when William Merrylees, an accomplished singer and violinist, was appointed precentor of the Lerwick Parish Church. Merrylees advanced the choral standards to include an anthem during the afternoon service.

In 1835 the Lerwick Subscription School was established, and lasted until 1844. Teachers were engaged from a religious sect known as Moravians. The last one was an Englishman called John Glass, an accomplished pianist and musical enthusiast. He was a hard taskmaster and had the choir practising five nights a week. Their first work was Mendelssohn's *Elijah*. The year was 1847, the same year that the work was first performed in Birmingham! Shetland was ahead of its time. After forming the choir he added a few instruments and there was the start of an orchestra.

1866 saw the ban on instrumental music in churches lifted and the pipe organ was installed in Lerwick Parish Church in 1871. The first organist was James Hunter, brother to R.B. Hunter, both of the Union Bank. He was to be followed by Mr Thomas Manson in 1881. Thomas Manson carried on the work of Merrylees and Glass with performances of *Messiah* and *Judas Maccabeus*, assisted by his sister Jemima at the piano. In 1883 the opening of the new Town Hall gave to a new focus for concerts and public occasions. Mr. Manson was the obvious choice to arrange the music to mark Queen Victoria's jubilee in 1887. There was a lot going on in Lerwick. A piano tuner came regularly from

Edinburgh, a professor came to give piano lessons and Thomas Manson opened a music and instrument department in the book and paper store.

In 1897 a group of string players had been making music under the leadership of Christie Gilbertson, calling themselves The Lerwick String Band. A notice in *The Shetland News* in March of that year advertises a concert by the Zetland Choir and String Band, pianist Miss Weldon and conductor Mr G. Paterson. The review continues: "Unfortunately irritating noise made by boys (and men) at the back of the hall, who when anything on the programme is not exactly to their taste, promptly "damn" it, then add insult to injury by encoring

1904, Orchestra. Top row: Hugh Tait, Wm. Nicolson, Wm. Peter Harrison, Christie Gilbertson (leader), Thos. Manson (conductor), Dr Willcock (patron), R. Mackay, A. J. Abernethy. Second row: Louisa Leisk, Dottie Sandison, Hattie Leask, Beatrice Hunter, Vanda Alger. Third row: Magnus Anderson, Gideon Stove, A. Murray. *(Courtesy of Shetland Museum)*

it." Sounded rather a riot! It continues: "Mr Gilbertson and his band deserve the hearty thanks and support of the musical public for their zealous efforts; and we hope, that the band may be soon made more complete." Around 1904 they asked Thomas Manson to be their conductor and with the addition of wind players became The Lerwick Amateur Orchestral Society.

The first advertisement we have, tempting us to a concert given by the Lerwick Amateur Orchestral Society. For 2/- one could reserve a seat at the Town Hall after consulting the seating plan.

It was a mixed concert, billed as classical, to include all sorts of music and playing.

The concert sounded like a great success to judge from *The Shetland News* review of 30th April, 1904:

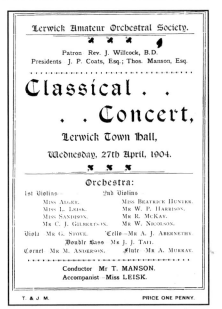

Saturday, 16th April, 1904, advert in *Shetland News* of a classical concert.
(Courtesy of Shetland Library)

1904 concert programme.
(Courtesy of Shetland Archives)

"A most delightful concert of orchestral music interspersed with a few vocal solos, was given in the Town Hall last Wednesday evening by the Lerwick Amateur Orchestral Society. This Society, founded a few years ago by some half-dozen enthusiasts, has done much excellent work at various entertainments in accompanying and playing a few numbers by themselves but this is the first occasion on which they have essayed such an ambitious thing as a classical concert composed almost entirely of orchestral music.

That attempted was more than justified, everyone present on Wednesday evening will, we are sure, admit. Of course as being the first orchestral concert given by local performers in Lerwick, it stands by itself so that there is really nothing to compare it with, but irrespective of this fact, there is no doubt what ever that for beautiful music, finished workmanship, and sustained interest, it stands out the best all round performance given in Lerwick for many a year, and will if we mistake not, be a standard from which future performances will be judged.

"The playing of the orchestra numbers all through was most credible to everyone taking part. The light and shade, the piános and fortes, the phrasing and the technical finish given to each piece played showed that both conductor and performers had been thoroughly in earnest over their work.

"Handel's overture to the Occasional Overture was perhaps an ambitious piece to attempt with a small orchestra but the performance showed more clearly than any of the numbers the abilities of the individual executants. The allegro movement is difficult demanding quick reading and nimble playing but it had gone through in splendid style.The three other movements especially the adagio were also played with a finish and taste that savoured little of the amateur. This overture, in the opinion of the people present was the finest in the whole programme, and received the best all-round rendering.

"The fantasia *Crown Diamonds* (Auber) played by the orchestra so pleased the audience that it had to be repeated in response to continued applause. The bright music received an exceedingly good rendering, being played with great technical exactness, spirit, and much fullness of tone in the loud passages, and fine taste in the pretty melodies it contains."

Let us look at some of the players involved, and what the *News* wrote about them.

Thomas Manson
Conductor 1904-1933

Thomas Manson was part of a musical family from Lerwick. Although he earned his living by printing and afterwards ownership of *The Shetland News* (a weekly newspaper) it was music that he loved. He started work as a printer at the age of 12.

He was 21 when he became organist in the Parish Church. The 1881 Kirk session wrote: "Several of the members spoke of Mr T. Manson as a most exemplary young man who had a excellent knowledge of music and who (with practice) would play the organ well". It was with some trepidation that Thomas took on the task — but who at that Kirk session meeting would have imagined that 60 years later he would still be there twice on Sundays and devoted to his daily practice at the age of 81.

His first teacher was David Sutherland, a watch maker from Unst, who taught him the sol-fa notation (more about David Sutherland's family later on). With his own money Thomas bought a harmonium to maintain constant practice at home.

He visited London on several occasions, to sing tenor at the Crystal Palace at the Handel festivals, along with 4,000 others.

Thomas Manson. *(Courtesy of T. M. Y. Manson)*

1907 letter to Thomas Manson to engage him as conductor. *(Courtesy of Shetland Archives)*

He was a natural leader and teacher. When the Lerwick String Band was looking for a conductor Mr W.P. Harrison, secretary, wrote asking Thomas Manson, an obvious choice, to join the group, for which he would be paid 2 guineas. (More than we pay the conductor today.)

Mr Manson was six feet in height, slim, long-legged with large hands. He possessed a commanding presence and kept the orchestra and choir inspired with his practice, demonstration, teaching and conducting. He taught singing in rural areas in the summer and had a ringing tenor voice as well as a complete falsetto. The choirs he conducted were amused when they were faced by a tall man with moustache singing soprano parts!

Something Shetland musicians could adopt today was when he urged instrumentalists to wiggle their big toe inside their shoe to make less noise when beating time.

It must be remembered that alongside this busy life Mr Manson wrote and published many books. These included *Humours of a Peat Commission, The Roll of Service* and *The Roll of Honour,* and *Lerwick during the Last Half Century.* Thomas Manson was a master printer and taught his employees to do the ornamental designs around programmes that were so fashionable at the time.

As the Lerwick Amateur Orchestral Society became more established some players began to accompany the Lerwick Amateur Opera Company, with

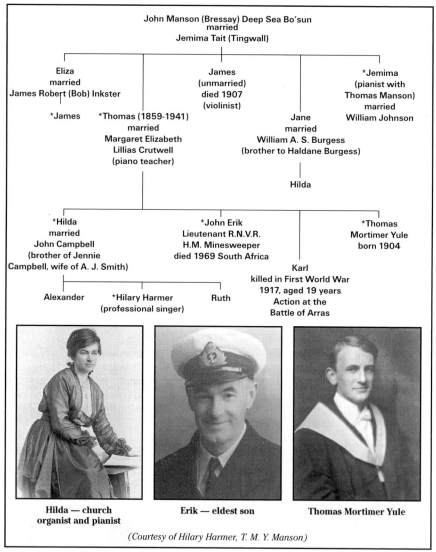

John Manson (Bressay) Deep Sea Bo'sun
married
Jemima Tait (Tingwall)

Eliza
married
James Robert (Bob) Inkster

James
(unmarried)
died 1907
(violinist)

*Jemima
(pianist with
Thomas Manson)
married
William Johnson

*James   *Thomas (1859-1941)
married
Margaret Elizabeth
Lillias Crutwell
(piano teacher)

Jane
married
William A. S. Burgess
(brother to Haldane Burgess)

Hilda

*Hilda
married
John Campbell
(brother of Jennie
Campbell, wife of A. J. Smith)

*John Erik
Lieutenant R.N.V.R.
H.M. Minesweeper
died 1969 South Africa

*Thomas
Mortimer Yule
born 1904

Karl
killed in First World War
1917, aged 19 years
Action at the
Battle of Arras

Alexander   *Hilary Harmer   Ruth
(professional singer)

Hilda — church
organist and pianist

Erik — eldest son

Thomas Mortimer Yule

(Courtesy of Hilary Harmer, T. M. Y. Manson)

The Manson family tree, * show connections with the orchestra.

many productions of Gilbert and Sullivan, conducted by Thomas Manson. The producer of these events was Mrs A. J. Smith (Miss Jean or Jennie Campbell).

Thomas Manson continued to play the organ at both Sunday services right up to his death, but he gave up the orchestra and opera in 1933 after a production of the *Mikado*.

Our next character is Gideon Stove. He came with his family to Lerwick at the age of five from North Roe. Gideon was a baker by trade but took the decision early on to study music full-time. He became an outstanding performer. Being born and bred in Shetland, he was very interested in the traditional fiddle tunes of his native islands and he collected and composed many tunes.

He had three sons: Magnus, who played and taught the violin alongside his full-time headship at the Mid Yell school; Harold, who was later to become a leader and soloist with the orchestra; and Alex, who worked in the Post Office and played with the orchestra. (Alex also played the accordion).

Gideon Stove.
(Courtesy of Magnus Stove)

Gideon was self-taught, which made his achievements all the more remarkable. He was teaching full-time and devoted the rest of the time to practice. Even when he reduced his personal performance he continued to teach. Many subsequent orchestra members benefitted, and could say they had been taught by such a genius. Gideon is said to have played a Stradivarius violin, brought back from the Mediterranean by his brother. Whatever it was, it had the most marvellous tone, and on the first occasion Mr Stove appeared as a violin soloist at an orchestral concert, the brilliance of his playing astounded the audience.

Christie Gilbertson was leader of the Lerwick Amateur Orchestral Society and founder of The Lerwick String Band. At this time he worked at the Post Office, and it must have been in conversation with other employees at the Post Office that the idea for the String Band was born. Not much more is known about Christie than that he later moved to Wick.

Vanda Sofia J. Alger was a daughter of Welsh Methodist minister, Rev. Joseph Bailey Alger, and Fanny Elizabeth Archbutt. Vanda was number three in a family of eight and married J. Flesher Rumfitt from South Africa. They emigrated with intentions to come back to Britain at some point, but never did.

The Shetland News wrote the following: "In a very difficult violin solo *Souvenirs D'Amerique* (Vieuxtemps) Miss Alger had ample scope for showing her technical skill to advantage. The piece demands rapid clean fingering, double stopping, the use of harmonics, and a very agile bow arm for the wide arpeggios. In each of these requirements Miss Alger showed a very agile bow

A tea party. Top row: Beatrice Hunter, Katie Donaldson, teacher Hayfield Cottage, Hattie Leask, ? ?,
Bessie Leask. Second row: Louisa Leisk, Jean Yule, Dottie Sandison, Mage Robertson (father built
Rocklea). *(Courtesy of Miss E. Durham)*

Louisa Leisk about 16 years of age.
(Courtesy of E. Durham)

Adelaide Beatrice Catherine Hunter.
(Courtesy of Shetland Museum)

Brass band members who were also members of the orchestra 1914-1915. Back row: J. J. Gifford, Willie Johnson, Sammy Scott, Sonny Smith, M. Macallum, L. G. (Lollie) Scott, A. W. Smith, L. A. Macallum, John Irvine, George Hay, Peter Goodlad, Herbert Goudie. Front row: Robert Mackay, Magnus Sutherland, W. G. Smith, Alexander Clark, McGowan Scott, Robert M. Y. Johnson, James Ratter, Laurence Stewart, Alexander Linklater. *(Courtesy of Shetland Museum)*

arm for the wide arpeggios and great proficiency, the harmonics especially being delightfully clear and fluty. From start to finish the piece was played with marked ability and the fair violinist received very hearty applause for her brilliant performance. Mrs Fanny Alger played the accompaniment with fine taste and finish."

Vanda had a sister that played but we shall come to her a little later.

Miss Hattie Leisk, and her sister Miss Louisa Leisk, were daughters of Provost John Leisk, Chairman of the Lerwick Harbour Trust. They lived at 169 Commerical Street, where Leisk and Sandison, draper and clothiers, were established in 1813. Louisa became Mrs. W.R. Durham, whose husband was Headmaster of the Central School. Hattie married Dr. James (Terry) Campbell.

Miss Beatrice Hunter was the daughter of James Hunter, and the niece of R.B. Hunter, both of the Union Bank (now the Bank of Scotland). She became a proficient violinist and gained her diploma. Miss Hunter took a teaching post in a girls' school in Stockholm, later to privately teach a wealthy Consul's family called Wicander.

During the Second World War she was in Sweden and during an attempt to get home had to travel via Russia, Siberia, Japan, Canada and the Atlantic.

The Wicander family asked Beatrice to return to Sweden to catalogue rare china that the family had bequeathed to a State Museum. Irvinesgord, her home at the south end of Lerwick (beside Quendale House and demolished to make way for the Lerwick Telephone Exchange), had a history behind it. The house was the town house of the Rev. John Turnbull, minister of Tingwall, and Sir Walter Scott visited him there in 1814.

Up-Helly-A' squad "Dutchies". Standing: W. Peter Harrison (merchant), R. C. Thomson (clerk), Peter Manson (farmer), Lollie Scott (draper), James Scott, Mackie Scott (ironmonger), John Robertson (Robertson's (Lerwick) Ltd). Front: William Robertson (farmer), G. K. Hunter (publican), John Robertson (R. & C. Robertson). Peter Manson was from Maryfield, Bressay; Lollie Scott, owner of Anderson & Co.; G. K. Hunter, owner of Vaults Bar. *(Courtesy of Shetland Museum)*

The Shetland News wrote of Miss Hunter's playing:

"A violin solo *Fantasia Pastorale* played by Miss Beatrice Hunter was a very excellent number. Miss Hunter has a fine style of playing and she takes out of the violin a full true tone even all through while her execution is clear clean and firm. Miss Hunter played the piece with great ability and was enthusiastically encored. In reply she played a pretty little piece which delighted the audience."

Mr W.P. Harrison began life as a draper with Anderson & Co., then after some years joined his father's business, a grocery shop, before starting his own hosiery business.

He was a very reliable and able player with the orchestra, playing well into the 1920s. His hobbies included angling and chess, and he was six years a member of the Harbour Trust. We have a good picture of him in an Up-Helly-A' squad.

Robert McKay was a long serving member of the Post Office, and received his Imperial Service Medal for 53 years of duty. He was a keen musician and accomplished violinist, a member of the Brass Band, and a Deacon at the U.F.

Church. He had a hearty manner, cheery and welcoming, athletically built and a very smart person. At one time he opened a confectionery shop in St. Olaf Street run by his wife. Bob McKay continued to play with the orchestra until 1947.

William Nicolson was the son of Captain Nicolson of the *S.S. St. Ninian*. He was not a strong child, delicate in health with lung disease. He worked as a law clerk but was forced to give up because of his chest. He attended art school in Edinburgh and was the artist who painted the portrait of Prime Minister Gladstone that once stood in the Town Hall, now in the care of the museum. Mr Nicolson was an excellent violin teacher with a delicate touch and a sympathetic command of his instrument. He gained an Associateship of the College of Violinists and used the letters A.C.V. after his name. Other members of the orchestra were his pupils and it must have been a loss when he died young from acute T.B. To add to his family's sadness his mother died the month before him.

The *News* reported:

"A very enjoyable number was the instrumental quartette *Come into the garden, Maud* played by Miss Leisk (piano), Mr W.E. Nicolson (first violin), Miss L. Leisk (second violin) and Mr A. J. Abernethey (cello). The tone produced by the various instruments was very pleasing and sweet and the performance kept well together".

Bob McKay and Jemima Hughson, centre, on their marriage day with Jemima's sister Jessie who married Fred Williamson far left. *(Courtesy of Bertha Martin)*

11

Abernethy Photographic Shop in Harbour Street. *(Courtesy of Shetland Museum)*

Andrew J. Abernethy was from Bridge of Walls. He came to Lerwick with his brother Arthur, who was eight years his senior, to set up a photographic business in Harbour Street. Andrew was interested in music and Arthur was a fine craftsman, making and repairing violins and bows. Andrew was well known for his gracious personality and quiet humour. He was married to Ruby Norholm from Scalloway. He died on 7th September, 1950.

Miss Dottie Sandison was the daughter of Alexander Sandison, a partner in Leisk and Sandison, and they lived in Auburn Cottage. Dottie married James Morrison around 1919, and left Shetland.

Her review in the *News* tells of:

"A promising soloist singing *A May Morning*, her voice mellow and sweet. Her annunciation good and she sings naturally and tastefully. She had an enthusiastic encore and in reply repeated two verses of the song".

Hugh Tait was another Post Office worker who later moved to Orkney and had a large family.

A. Murray was a banker about whom little is known.

Magnus Anderson was a tailor who came to Shetland when the fishing was good. He came from Peterhead and stayed for a while, before moving back to Peterhead. He then visited Shetland regularly, staying at Glenfarquhar for about a week at a time to collect orders with "New seasons materials: Orders respectfully solicited", as advertised in *The Shetland News*.

1906 Orchestra. Back row: A. Abernethy, A. Murray, ?, W. P. Harrison, Dr Willcock, Magnus Anderson, Bob MaKay, Gideon Stove, Magnus Sutherland, Hugh Tait. Front row: Dorothy Sandison, Christie Gilbertson (leader), Miss Weldon, Thomas Manson, Louisa Leisk.
(Courtesy of Shetland Museum)

"The cornet solo *Killarney* played by Mr Magnus Anderson was the most enjoyable number, a lovely melody which received full justice from Mr Anderson's tone. The tone brought out being sweet broad and sympathetic, the audience demanded repetition which forced Mr Anderson to concede."

The Patron of the Lerwick Orchestra was Dr Willcock O.B.E., M.A., D.D., D.Litt, F.R.H.S., an enthusiastic supporter. He spent 49 years as minister of St. Ringan's Church. Originally from Liverpool, he married Annie Malcolmson, a teacher of French, German, English Literature and Music. They had three sons. It was largely from his work that funds were made available to build St Ringan's.

Dr Willcock was a very active man: President of the Lerwick Choral Union, founder of the Boys' Brigade, active in the Soldiers & Sailors Family Association, and patron of the Lerwick Amateur Orchestral Society. He had a great love of music but was not a performer himself.

He heartily enjoyed Gilbert and Sullivan and was a friend of Thomas Manson. They studied the Bible together. Dr Willcock also gave "Penny Readings" in the Town Hall. These were readings at which the public were charged an entrance fee of one penny.

In proposing a vote of thanks after the 1904 concert, Dr Willcock wished: "Long life and prosperity to the society. To attain this they needed recruits of the right sort. There were some departments that the orchestra would like to strengthen, some instruments might be added like the clarinet and oboe which would be effective if properly handled".

Mr Manson asked the audience to give a vote of thanks to Miss Leisk the accompanist; it was not so long ago that he had been amazed at the ease and ability with which she had taken up and performed the very difficult and onerous work falling to her. She was always there and always correct. She deserved the greatest applause for her work in connection with this concert.

Perhaps this quote from *The Shetland News* can sum up the feeling in the town in April 1904:

"On all hands there is but one

Magnus Sutherland.
(Courtesy of Shetland Museum)

voice in regard to it, that the voice giving expression to a feeling akin to astonishment that a small town like Lerwick, there exists so much executive talent, talent now so organised and trained that it can attempt and adequately perform music by the best masters. The feeling in Lerwick today is one of keen pride in its orchestra and there is no doubt that Lerwegians will appreciate and encourage it further after hearing the excellent performance of Wednesday evening. The audience which was a fairly large one was thoroughly appreciative and we can imagine it was a most enjoyable one to play and sing to."

In 1906 another photograph of the orchestra was taken, Magnus Sutherland having joined them.

Magnus, Julia and Annie Sutherland were from the Sutherland family in Colvadale, Unst. Their father and mother were Thomas and Joan Sutherland. Thomas was a brother to David Sutherland, the well known watchmaker. David built the house referred to as the House of David, now the Department of Social Work office in St Olaf Street.

David Sutherland, you might recall, taught Thomas Manson music. One amusing story about David, that has nothing to do with the orchestra, is that at the Coronation of King George V he was playing tunes on the Town Hall clock. To the dismay of folk gathered they were the *Red Flag* and other socialist tunes. When told to play something suitable he played *That's the way the money goes, Pop goes the Weasel*!

Back now to the Orchestra! The brothers David and Thomas were very close and married two sisters, Ann and Joan Nisbet. Thomas helped his brother in the watchmaking business as well as being a stonemason.

Magnus H. Sutherland was the son of Thomas, and took a keen interest in the Lerwick Amateur Orchestral Society, the Brass Band and a group which met and played in St Ringan's Church. He also taught the violin. Magnus provided the music for the North Star cinema first with his violin and later with records. He married Anne Cheyne but the marriage was not a long one as Anne died of T.B. at the age of 28 years.

Magnus showed a keen interest in all mechanical objects and had the ability, like his uncle, to fit and mend things. The whole family were outstanding knitters of fine lace and Magnus had a part-time job dressing Shetland lace with his mother-in-law, Mrs Laurence Robertson. It was a real tragedy when Magnus lost the power of his arm due to a stroke at the age of 47 years, and was subsequently unable to play the violin. He died four years later, in 1937.

More about the two Sutherland sisters later on.

Lerwick
Amateur Orchestral Society.

PROGRAMME
OF
ORCHESTRAL CONCERT
IN THE
TOWN HALL,
WEDNESDAY, March 23, 1910

Conductor, - - Mr THOS. MANSON.
Accompanist, - - Miss HILDA MANSON.

T. & J. MANSON PRINTERS LERWICK   **ONE PENNY.**

Gilbert and Sullivan Operas

In the 1920s the Lerwick Amateur Orchestral Society held a meeting to discuss policy. John Erik Manson, son of Thomas Manson, was now involved, playing the violin. He was also the secretary at this point.

A difference of opinion was emerging. There was a group of players who wanted to prepare for a public concert and another which was in favour of practising for perfection's sake. The meeting decided to put the instruments up for sale and wind up the society. Shortly after this Mr A.R.M. Mathewson bought the instruments in order to keep them together in one place.

Thomas Manson had been conducting opera with the Lerwick Musical Society for some time and orchestral members joined him. A group at St. Ringan's Church continued to play at Christmas time services. Gilbert and Sullivan was a firm favourite with the Shetland public and, under the baton of Thomas Manson, appeared almost yearly. In 1933 the *Mikado* was performed and it was to be the last opera with Thomas Manson. He suffered an attack of laryngitis during the winter of 1933-34 and was never again to coach the company.

G. & S. nucleus of orchestra in the 1920s. Back row: George Hay, Thomas Manson, Mrs Jas. Campbell, Jim Stephen. Front row: Gideon Stove, Annie Sutherland, Andrew Abernethy, Allie Linklater, Julia Sutherland, Erik Manson. *(Courtesy of Magnus Stove)*

Past reviews in *The Shetland News* give us an insight to the concerts. They are particularly detailed because of the connection between the Manson family and the newspaper. In 1927 the *Pirates of Penzance* was a success for the orchestra. Dr Crawford, County Medical Officer of Health, spoke to give thanks. About the orchestra he said: "He would not say that previous performances of the orchestra had been above criticism; but he would say most emphatically that their finished playing on this occasion had done so much to make the performance such a complete success."

The advertisement in the papers requests the "audience to be seated by 7.50pm for the 8pm start" (not something we achieve today). Also "it is requested that Ladies remove hats during the performance".

The characters that took part in the Gilbert and Sullivan Operas were to include Gideon Stove, whom we have spoken about.

Next is John Erik Manson, son of Thomas Manson, who entered the printing works and was instrumental with his father in producing the *Shetland Roll of Honour* and the *Shetland Roll of Service* books, which were awarded the Hood Medal from the British print magazine for the best work of the year by a small firm in Britain. Erik, as he was known, conducted a Gilbert and Sullivan in 1921, *Trial by Jury*, and played in most others. He was an officer in the First World War and in the South African Navy during the Second War. In 1929 he and his family emigrated to South Africa for a better life and sun for his delicate son.

**Mrs A. J. Smith (Jennie Campbell) producer of
Gilbert & Sullivan opera.**
(Courtesy of Douglas Smith)

Erik Manson.
(Courtesy of Shetland Museum)

Alex Linklater was a cheerful and popular man who had a shop called the Shetland Hosiery Company. Part of it was in what is now the Shetland Times Bookshop, selling hosiery and drapery, and part at 102 Commercial Street. He was a keen Brass Band man and performed in the St Ringan's Christmas Day concerts.

Annie and Julia Fraser Sutherland were sisters of Magnus and nieces to David Sutherland of Unst. Annie was a gentle and unobtrusive woman with a passion for music. She played in the second violin section and then moved to the first. Whatever part she played she played with taste and skill. She devoted much of her spare time to music and so it must have been

Alex Clark, Alex Linklater and McGowan Scott.
(Courtesy of Capt. Malcolm Linklater)

a loss to the orchestra when in 1927 she went into hospital for an operation and died.

Julia Fraser Sutherland went on to play with the orchestra into the late 1950s. Living in Chromate Lane and being so experienced with Shetland knitting she was well known in and around the town.

George Hay was a cooper by trade, working at the Bloomfield site on the North Road. He came from Fraserburgh and had two daughters. One daughter, Elise, married a man in Shetland called Ian McKenzie. Ian's sister married Joseph Linklater, a member we shall meet later. George was Brass Band master from about 1930-1939. He left for Fraserburgh about 1939.

James A. Stephen was born in Scalloway in 1903. The family moved to Lerwick in 1910, residing at the Esplanade House. He served his apprenticeship as a marine engineer with Macleod and Maclean. He went to sea as an engineer with the City Line. After a shore appointment in Bristol he followed his older brother in 1949 to Vancouver, where he lives today. He married Miss Ena Smith of Craigielea, St Olaf Street, and has two sons. Apart

Patience Gilbert and Sullivan opera, 1926. Back row: W. Anderson, A. Coutts, L. Dalziel, W. Smith, M. MacLean, J. Hunter, S. Anderson. Second row: A. Garriock, N. Smith, M. Anderson, A. Smith, F. Campbell, T. Pottinger, J. Ramsay, W. Watt, B. Tulloch, E. Robertson, L. Dalziel. Third row: G. Hay, D. Sinclair, A. Abernethy, J. J. Brown, K. Gray, E. S. Reid Tait, Mrs Marshall, W. Smith, Mrs Jas. Campbell, R. Hughson, Allie Linklater, Jim Stephen. Front row: Julia Sutherland, Thomas Manson, Annie Sutherland, Erik Manson, Gideon Stove. *(Courtesy of Capt. M. Linklater)*

from his musical interest he is a great enthusiast of Up-Helly-A' and was a keen footballer, playing for Lerwick Thistle. Mr. Stephen is an uncle to Mr. Magnus Shearer and Mrs. Noelle Gordon.

The review from *The Shetland News* of the opera *Patience*, performed in the Town Hall on 1st- 6th March was as follows: "Performances began on what turned out to be one of the worst nights of the year with heavy rain and high winds but the audience, although small was most appreciative and enthusiastic. After the overture had been rendered by the orchestra the opera succeeded to delight the audience. The orchestra was composed of strings on this occasion. The only wind instrument this time being a cornet performed the difficult task of accompanying with full and complete sympathy, never obtruding itself but giving the support needed. In accompanist Mrs Jas Campbell was everything an accompanist should be, skilful sympathetic and watchful. Mr Manson conducted in his usual carefree and able manner."

A list of the performances given by The Lerwick Musical Society is quite impressive;

1914	*Pirates of Penzance*	1926	*Patience*
1921	*Trial by Jury*	1927	*Pirates of Penzance*
1922	*Mikado*	1928	*Sorcerer*
1923	*Iolanthe*	1931	*The Princess of Poppyland*
1924	*Gondoliers*	1932	*Iolanthe*
1925	*H.M.S. Pinafore*	1933	*Mikado*

A. R. M. Mathewson
Conductor 1936-1944 & 1950-1955

When Mr Mathewson became conductor of the orchestra in 1936 it had been inactive for some years. Players had met together in the Gilbert and Sullivan works and with the St. Ringan's Church group.

Provost Smith, Andrew Abernethy, Eva Alger, and others discussed the prospect of re-starting the orchestra at a meeting in the ante room of the Town Hall on 20th November, 1936. "Orkney have one and they saw no reason why Shetland should not," was the comment. Miss Alger had formed a small orchestra in previous years and it had been very much appreciated at various functions. She thought an excellent orchestra could be formed with Mr Mathewson as conductor.

At this point Mr Mathewson stated that he had eight instruments which he bought in the 1920s from the sale of the orchestra equipment and was very willing to allow these to be used. He also had over 200 orchestral scores which he would present to the society.

The meeting was then unanimous in favour of forming a society and the committee consisted of: A. R. M. Mathewson, Mrs C. Kean, McGowan Scott, Miss E. Alger, A. W. Smith, Miss Chrissie Watt, R. M. Y. Johnson, R. A. Inkster.

Practice night was Friday in St Clement's Hall. Miss Kean became pianist and Mrs Watt deputy.

A. R. M. (Ronnie) Mathewson was obviously the main driving force behind the venture. Thomas Manson and his younger son Mortimer had been invited but they had a prior engagement, and could not attend. Ronnie was the son of a Yell man. He had music lessons from Professor Donald Tovey in Edinburgh. He gave a false age to join the Gordon Highlanders in the First World War, only to be wounded in the trenches. He then did what he enjoyed most: entertaining the troops. Returning to Shetland he worked in the Post Office

A. R. M. Mathewson. *(Courtesy of Mrs M. Walker)*

and later was Burgh Chamberlain, a post he held until he retired. We must assume, however, that most of his spare time was taken up with music. He wrote songs, arranged musical shows, and adapted parts for the available players of the orchestra to match their ability. (Our present conductor does this, and he will confirm how time consuming it is.) This was alongside performances with a band called The Players.

Concerts and practice continued until early 1940s with various people coming and going. Someone who was to be a cornerstone of the orchestra until 1992 came on the scene in 1936. This was Dr. T.M.Y. Manson, son of Thomas Manson, brother of Erik, and a flute player.

Again back to the *News* and a report of the Orchestral Concert 20th April, 1939.

"The Lerwick Amateur Orchestral Society submitted a concert in the Town Hall of light orchestral music supplemented by vocal and instrumental

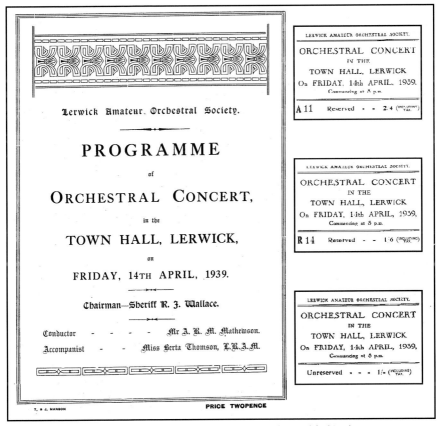

1939 programme and tickets. *(Courtesy of Shetland Archives)*

pieces. Evidence of the keen interest felt throughout the town in the concert was shown by the audience who gathered in every seat bar a few at the back. Mr A.R.M. Mathewson, conductor, had succeeded in raising the personnel of the orchestra to 20, a very credible number for a small town. Moreover it is a very complete body with woodwind, brass as well as the string family being represented. The result was that colour, variety and tone which makes good orchestral music so enjoyable was present and it allowed an adequate rendering of the numbers submitted.

"The concert was an enjoyable one with orchestra pieces not too high brow. The scene was supplemented by a number of interesting vocal numbers. The bill of fare present appealed to every taste and made up a very successful evenings entertainment.

"Before the National Anthem was sung Mr Manson proposed a hearty vote of thanks to Mr Mathewson, the orchestra, the singers and reciter and the accompanist for a very enjoyable and remarkable concert they had given, which had been especially noticeable for the precision and clean cut-off in their playing. This orchestra, he said was a continuation of the orchestra founded in Lerwick 40 or 50 years ago and which continued for a number of years. It was now in quite good condition very efficient and it was for the public to maintain and encourage such an institution by adequately supporting it by full attendance at its concert as was done that night.

"Mr Mathewson returning thanks, expressed admiration of Mr Manson's praise, which he particularly valued and of the splendid support given to the orchestra by the public. He thanked the accompanist Miss Thomson for what she had done. Mr Mathewson appealed to parents in the town to send their children to music lessons no matter what the instrument chosen. He could easily, he said, place many more instrumentalists in the orchestra than those already there. He never regretted the hard struggle he had in the early years with his music teacher who was present in the hall that night. He had had a great deal of pleasure out of music and parents could do no better that send their children to music teachers. Mr Mathewson concluded by reiterating his thanks to Mr Manson and the audience after which the National Anthem was led by the orchestra. The proceeds of the concert were in aid of orchestra funds."

Other players included Miss Eva Alger (sister to Vanda) founder member and instrumental in reviving the orchestra in 1936. She had a musical mother, an accomplished pianist, who nonetheless could not stretch an octave. Miss Eva Alger gave lessons in Lystina House and latterly Annsbrae House. She never married and died in 1938 and left all her music to the Lerwick Orchestra.

John S. Johnson was secretary to a Medical Insurance Company.

John (Jack) Goodlad was a long serving member of the orchestra who lived in Union Street. He was well known for his small musical groups at the

Kathleen V. Scott, née Alger, Phyllis Rumfitt (step-daughter to Vanda Alger), Eva Lillian Alger, Kathleen Scott, later Robertson. *(Courtesy of Mr Frank Scott)*

house, and his kind hospitality. He ran the shoe shop Goodlad and Goodlad. His teacher was Magnus Sutherland.

Our next quote from the *News* (1939) is: "Tom Anderson who played a solo of Scottish selections went far to establish a reputation as a violinist of very marked ability and was warmly encored."

Dr Tom Anderson was a well known fiddler, founder of the Forty Fiddlers, and collector of tunes all around Shetland while doing his job as an insurance agent. He was a composer of music and promoter of music from Shetland. He received an M.B.E. for services to music. It is interesting that Tom's first lesson had been secondhand, so to speak, from a man who had taken a lesson from Gideon Stove.

David Robertson. A cooper by trade and uncle to Miss Bertha Robertson.

Miss Bertha Robertson. Long standing member of the orchestra, who played well into the 1990s. She held various committee positions and would likely be found sitting beside Miss Jessie McMillan. Bertha married Mr George Gray.

Miss Jessie McMillan also played into the 1990s. She had been a pupil of Miss Eva Alger, taking lessons in Lystina House. Jessie worked for a number of years in the Hay & Co. offices. Bertha and Jessie became known as Mutt & Jeff after the newspaper cartoon. Bertha married Mr Sidney Leask.

Jack Goodlad.
(Courtesy of Mr Peter Goodlad)

Miss E.H. (Nellie) Smith, was a schoolmaster's daughter from Cunningsburgh, and a teacher herself.

The Shetland News, 1939: "By no-means the least interesting number on the programme was the duet for two piano forte played by accompanist Bertha Thompson, L.R.A.M., and Mr Ronnie Mathewson, both having a very high standard of proficiency and the delight and manner in which they performed the two duets called for enthusiastic applause and instant demands for an encore."

Mr Frank Garriock, latterly Norwegian consul, played as a young man on a few occasions and had tuition from Miss Alger.

Henry Hurlock began working in a butcher's shop and from about 1940 worked in the Labour Exchange. He was a very familiar sight with his double bass and played for many years. He also held the post of treasurer and secretary. Along with the orchestra he played with the Robertsons' Dance Band.

Mrs George Gray (Bertha Robertson)
(Courtesy of Mrs Vera Polson)

Mrs Sidney Leask, with Miss Alger's violin (Jessie McMillan). *(Courtesy of Douglas Grant)*

Mr A. D. (Sandy) Bennett was a physical education teacher and later had a hosiery business called Shetland Wools where the shop Rig Out is now. Mr Bennett's wife was a sister to Dr. Durham of Scalloway. He moved south in 1967 and lives in Callender.

**The New Players: T. T. Leask, Bobby Garriock, D. K. Gilbertson,
Tom Anderson, Willie Johnson and Billy Kay.** *(Courtesy of Mr Billy Kay)*

T. T. Leask, a talented musician, played saxophone in the dance band called The New Players with Billy Kay, Bobby Garriock, Dave Gilbertson, Tom Anderson and Peerie Willie Johnson. He worked as a shop assistant in D. and G. Kays. He played clarinet in the orchestra but could turn out a tune on the fiddle.

McGowan Scott's father was Captain Scott of the North boats, who had 11 sons and one daughter. Captain Scott would. recount, much to the suprise of his passengers, how he had 11 sons and each one had a sister. Mr Scott junior had a very fine voice and it was considered that he sang at the expense of his other talents. (He could play the clarinet, among other things.) His son, Jack Scott, was later to play in

R. M. Y. Johnson.
(Courtesy of Mrs H. Gould)

the orchestra. Another brother was Lolly G. Scott who married Kathleen Alger, sister to Eva and Vanda. Lolly was a keen Brass Band player.

R. M. Y. Johnson, editor of *The Shetland Times*, was a gifted musician and could play many instruments. His main one was the piano. He often felt frustrated because players would not practise each week. They would come just at concert time and playing was not always up to standard. He would bring an organ to fill in the difficult parts.

The question of charging for a performance at any function was discussed and it was decided on the motion of Mr McGowan Scott, seconded by Mr R. M. Y. Johnson, to fix this at £1-1/- per night.

The War Years

During the Second World War many men and women were away from Shetland, thus depleting the normal pool of players. However, service men came to Shetland and wanted something to do in their spare evenings. Some longlasting friendships were made.

Sgt Ronald G. Popperwell was brought to Shetland during the war because he could speak French, only to find on arrival here he was to "vet" Norwegian volunteers and refugees arriving with the "Shetland Bus". Undaunted, he learnt Norwegian rapidly, and this was to be the staple of his later career as head of Department of Scandinavian Studies at Cambridge University. Ronald Popperwell is remembered for riding around Shetland on his motor bike in the blackout with his violin case strapped to his back, joining in the musical life of Lerwick.

He came from Essex, his first job being in an insurance office. His ambition was to be a professional violinist, and he became A.R.C.M. in 1936. Shetland remained a lifelong enthusiasm and he returned many times over the years to play with the orchestra until his death in 1983.

Geoffrey I. de Mercado was a professional violinist, having been taught by Henry Holst. He had played in the London Symphony Orchestra and with the Lyons Corner House, as well as with the Universal Philharmonic Orchestra. When the war came he joined up and after a period in Norfolk (playing with the Steve Race Dance Band) he was posted to various places,

Ronald G. Popperwell.
(Courtesy of Miss I. Morris)

including Sudan. He changed from music to meteorology as the war progressed, and this was the profession he eventually returned to after the war, finding music rather dull now. (Lyons Corner House was not as exciting as the palace in Khartoum!)

Mr de Mercado was posted to the Meteorological Observatory in Lerwick in about 1946, and the orchestra was very keen to have him join them. It is interesting to note here that Mr de Mercado felt that: "The biggest and most important name, although he had died when I arrived, was Gideon Stove. I have no doubt that many string players had been taught by, and had all their musical grounding, by the late Mr Stove."

After a spell at the Met Office in Lerwick he was posted to the Middle East. Mr de Mercado returned to Shetland in 1950. In 1958 he had taken a part-time post as music teacher with the schools, travelling from Brae to

G. I. de Mercado.
(Courtesy of Mr de Mercado

Sandwick. One of his achievements was forming a youth orchestra in Scalloway. He left Shetland in 1969 to work in Arbroath, where he lives today, following his first love, natural history.

There had been a move at this point to amalgamate the Choir and Orchestra calling it, The Choral and Orchestral Society of Lerwick. It was the Orchestra that did not feel able to join in respect of their few numbers and proficiency.

G. I. de Mercado's youth orchestra, mid-1960s. Mr Lees (The County Music Organiser on right).
(Courtesy of G. I. de Mercado)

Post War Conductors

Miss Jean P. Boyd, L.R.A.M.
Conductor 1945-1947

Miss Boyd was a teacher at the Central School and founder of the Music Festival in Shetland. Quite a few concerts were undertaken under the leadership of Miss Boyd. During the Thanksgiving Week in 1945 a combined concert with the choral society was held, setting the pattern for a number of concerts over the years held by the combined forces of Orchestra and Choral Society. Other performances were Haydn's *The Seasons* and Gounod's *Faust*.

In 1947 she conducted a large choir in the Town Hall. As our review in *The Shetland News* tells us, it was on the worst night of the year for weather. A number of singers did not arrive from Scalloway, and the tenor soloist could not get up from the south. This must have been a nightmare for the groups involved but at that time they were lucky enough to have Mr P. Shuldham-Shaw in Shetland and as well as playing of the oboe he sang the tenor part. Dr Manson recalls that Handel must have known that one day the oboist would

Miss Jean P. Boyd. *(Courtesy of Miss Boyd)*

have to sing the tenor part in the *Messiah*, as the two parts did not overlap but were quite separate. Mr Shuldham-Shaw was a collector of folk songs.

Despite the weather the audience was a packed one, with extra seats brought in. Mr J.R.S. Clark, president of the Choral, made a series of announcements. After telling the audience about the 10 singers that were missing and the change of soloist he went on to say: "This was the first time that the orchestra had participated with the choral in a full accompaniment including the solos, and the first time for the *Messiah* with full accompaniment in Lerwick. All the string parts were represented tonight, totalling 15 players in all, with Miss Mary Garriock at the piano. The orchestra received general commendation, mixed with knowledgeable criticism. All comment was unanimous on the orchestra's improvement and that it had made a big improvement on the choir's performances. Chief honours go to Miss Boyd who arduously trained the choir and orchestra over the winter. The audience gave Miss Boyd a special ovation on her leaving the hall."

New faces in the Orchestra included:

Mary Garriock, a music teacher at the Anderson Educational Institute and a perfectionist at the piano and organ.

Freddie Tait, Glasgow University graduate, pilot with B.O.A.C., flew jumbo jets, and transported Princess Anne on her honeymoon.

James M. Spence, a physical education and primary teacher, latterly Headmaster in Aberdeenshire.

In 1948 Mr Mathewson again took on the post as conductor. Many successful concerts were given. During 1948 Community Week a concert was performed in the Garrison Theatre, with music such as Haydn's *Clock Symphony*, Edward German's *Merry England, Eine Kleine Nachtimusik* by Mozart, and excerpts from Smetana's *The Bartered Bride*. Yearly concerts took place, usually in the Garrison Theatre. Programmes were rising in price; they now cost sixpence and the proceeds went to Society funds.

A note in the "minute book" for a committee meeting at this time is amusing. "A motion is put forward to allow 10 minutes for smoking during a practice night." I wonder what effect this had on the wind players ability to blow?

People performing in these concerts included some we have already met: John Goodlad, Tom Anderson,

Messiah **programme 1947.**
(Courtesy of Douglas Johnstone)

Messiah 1947 Concert in Town Hall. Orchestra (left to right): Mary Garriock, Tom Anderson, John Goodlad, Beatrice Hunter, William Sandison, Fred Tait, T. M. Y. Manson, Sandy Bennet, James Spence, Julia Sutherland, Robert Mackay and Elizabeth Smith. Choral members (top row): Jim Clark, Mimi Peterson, Anna Brown (Robertson), Jessie Smith, Nell Harrison, Jennie Gray, Miss Garriock, Daisy Conochie, Bill Rhind (????), Stewart Smith and Willie Anderson. Second row: Cissie Smith, Frances Smith, Mrs Petrie, Joan Brain, Peter Robertson, Tom Pottinger, Mervin Jones, Murdo MacLean, Lissie Ratter, Geira Burgess, Lena Mouat, Mollie Odie, W. Robertson and John Manson. Front row: Hetty Robertson, Elizabeth Barclay, Marjorie Manson, Mrs Attie Smith, Eddie Henry, P. Shuldham-Shaw, Doris Hunter, Miss Boyd, Maggie Blance, Ronald Robb, Kitty Gray, L. Sinclair, J. Rogerson, A. W. Smith and Lolly Dalziel. *(Courtesy of Mrs H. Hurlock)*

Bertha Gray, Jessie Leask, Nellie Smith, Julia Sutherland, Joe Linklater, Henry Hurlock, Mortimer Manson, Sandy Bennet, Thomas Leask, James M Spence.

Others were Harold Stove (son of Gideon Stove), Mrs J. Dalziel (or, before she married, Miss Mimie Shearer), the orchestra's accompanist until 1961, Alex O'Neill, R. C. G. (Robbie) Laurenson, a Customs man, J. D. Wilson, Drew Robertson, music teacher and present Brass Band Master, and Alex (Sonny) Irvine, caretaker at Montfield Hospital.

Mr D. K. Gilbertson was a member of the Brass Band as well as the orchestra. He enjoyed music very much. His working life was spent in Tulloch of Shetland, latterly as a director. He died in 1994 at the age of 81.

Harold Stove
(Courtesy of Douglas Smith)

Bertha Thomson, pianist and teacher at the Central School, married the son of Admiral Max Horton. C. W. Arthur, registrar, and A. W. (Wilfred) Smith, uncle to Douglas Smith. He was a cooper by trade but worked with the fishing and owned property around the town.

Joseph L. Linklater, Brass Band Master who at one time worked for William Johnson (Radio Bill) of Johnson Cottage. Radio Bill had the shop on Commercial Street where Swanson's now is. After that he worked in the Further Education Office before he went to New Zealand.

In 1949 two concerts were given, one in January and one in May. This must have been a strain on the performers, but does show the hard work Mr Mathewson put into the orchestra, and the standard the orchestra had reached.

A selection from Gounod's *Faust* was played in 1950, and later that year *Geirhilda*, a Norse-Shetland drama by D. H. Sandison of Nesting was

Mr D. K. Gilbertson.
(Courtesy of Mrs Silk)

Mr and Mrs A. W. Smith. *(Courtesy of Douglas Smith)*

performed during the first Viking Congress, which had been organised at the Shetland end by Dr. Manson. *God Save the King* was played and was followed by the national anthems of all the other countries present at the Congress.

An Orchestral Concert in the Garrison Theatre 14th April, 1951 brought this review in the *News*:

"Two features of special interest in the concert by the Lerwick Orchestra under A. R. M. Mathewson — the appearance of Mr G. I. de Mercado, as leader

William Johnson Jr., Joe Linklater and Willie Johnson (Radio Bill) playing records in the Gilbertson Park. *(Courtesy of Shetland Museum)*

and solo violinist and the welcome sound of three cellos to enrich the orchestra. The woodwind was at its average strength with one each of the main instruments and the brass section, without a tenor trombone leaving the trumpet and bass trombone to fill in. Mrs J. Dalziel on the piano helped to make up the want of bassoon and horn. Twenty players all told. Apart from frequent out of tuneness in the wind section reports about the concert were good. An interesting and varied programme was played. At the close Baillie G. H. Burgess eloquently thanked the orchestra, conductor and Mr de Mecardo as well as the two lady cellists playing in the orchestra for the first time — Mrs Dr. Yule now of Lerwick and Mrs Neven-Spence down from Uyeasound especially for the occasion. Mr Mathewson thanked the orchestra and the boys of the Boys' Brigade and Boy Scouts for ushering and the programmes."

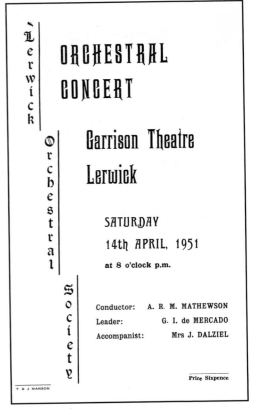

Lerwick Orchestral Society

ORCHESTRAL CONCERT

Garrison Theatre
Lerwick

SATURDAY
14th APRIL, 1951
at 8 o'clock p.m.

Conductor: A. R. M. MATHEWSON
Leader: G. I. de MERCADO
Accompanist: Mrs J. DALZIEL

Price Sixpence

T & J MANSON

An Orchestral Concert in the Garrison Theatre.
(Courtesy of Lerwick Orchestra)

Helly Hoy came in April 1952. This was a concert of light entertainment written by Ronnie Mathewson and Harry Kay, performed in the Garrison Theatre, in aid of the Lerwick Orchestral funds and the Shetland Sports Association. Harry Kay took the leading part of Major Hock, famous Mining engineer. The orchestra earned £75 at this very popular concert.

From *The Shetland News*, Wednesday, 16th April: "The eagerly awaited *Helly Hoy* featuring the renowned Major Hock, renowned mining engineer daring the dangers of the Shetland dialect was in the Garrison Theatre. The promised "uplowsin" is on, with no sign of a "brak" in the delight of the audience who are nightly crowding the Theatre. Mr Harry Kay has been the creator of Helly Hoy and wrote most of the libretto, which has been most successful and will be remembered for a long time. Despite his long absence from Shetland he has not forgotten the dialect, colour or tone. Sharing the honours were the orchestra and its inimitable conductor Mr Mathewson. No

Photograph *Helly Hoy*. Back row: Harold Mathewson, Bill Carter, Tom Leask, Tom Georgeson, Tom Pottinger, Jack Scott, Alex Irvine, Dave Gilbertson. Second row: Willie Johnson, Douglas Smith, T. M. Y. Manson, Ronald Conochie, Nellie Smith, ?, Jack Goodlad, Julia Sutherland, Bertha Gray, Jessie McMillan, Bill Sandison, Betty and Sheila Mundie, Dolly Anderson, Stewart Smith, Joan Stevenson, Edie Henry, Greta Coutts, Tom Anderson, Georgie Rhind, Harriet Mathewson, ?, Dr Yule, James Smith, Joe Linklater. Front row: Greta Gifford, Minnie Wright, Leila Young, George Burgess, A. R. M. Mathewson, Harry Kay, Alex Gray, Marjory Barclay, Mona Smith, Jessie Smith.   (*Courtesy of Mr Billy Kay*)

one will ever know the tremendous highly skilled work done by Mr Mathewson, who is responsible for all the orchestrations and harmonies and wrote out the entire score for Mr Billy Kay to photograph in order to get the necessary copy."

Then again on Wednesday, 23rd April: "Now unfortunately only a memory, but a very happy one, the amazing popular and successful Shetland show called *Helly Hoy* ended its record eight night run on Monday evening. If possible it ended on a higher note than it began, for each night the inimitable Major Hock and his lively company and accomplished orchestra went from success to success and provided bright and breezy entertainment and unlimited humour for some 2,500 people young and old alike."

HELLY HOY!

Here's a kolishang if ever dey wir wan! Nearly half a hunder songs, choruses, whartettes, duets an' a half daft minin' major.

Major Hock

blasted sky high by the Lerwick Orchestra

You never heard d'lik o'it! an aa strung tigidder wi a treed it aye keeps brakin. Horns an' looder horns, strings an' floots 15 hunderweight a pianos, no end a sherg an' Shetland sheeks.

Conductor: A. R. M. Mathewson.
Leader: G. de Mercado.
Accompanists: Mrs J. Dalziel; W. R. D. Kay

Garrison Theatre
12th to 19th April

In aid of Lerwick Sports Association and Lerwick Orchestral Society

Turn ower da pages fur twartree o da wirds

1952 programme. *(Courtesy of Shetland Archives)*

1955 Miss Iris Loveridge Concert

A. R. M. Mathewson was an ambitious man and in April 1955 he organised a concert in the Garrison Theatre for full orchestra and two visiting professional artists: Hilary Campbell, a soprano and granddaughter of Thomas Manson, and Iris Loveridge, a pianist from London. Much work went into the arrangements both with the travel, administration, and of course, practice. Twenty orchestral players took part in this two day event. An oboist was brought from Aberdeen University Orchestra, a clarinettist from Kirkwall and a trumpet player from the Gordon Highlanders Regiment. *The Shetland News* review was good, and the audience enjoyed the concert, but it was felt that perhaps the orchestra had over-stretched itself. By all accounts it had spent a lot of money, £40, plus all expenses to bring Miss Loveridge north, not an unreasonable amount but a lot for a small place like Shetland.

It must have been a terrific experience for the local players to take part in. The piano used was an upright one and perhaps not what Miss Loveridge was used to. She spent some time during the next few years encouraging the Education Department to buy its first grand. The music was quite difficult. In particular, the *Dance of the Comedians* from the *Bartered*

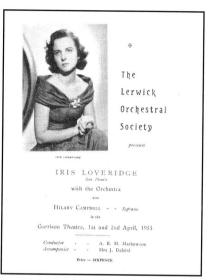

The Lerwick Orchestral Society

presents

IRIS LOVERIDGE
Solo Pianist

with the Orchestra

also

HILARY CAMPBELL - - *Soprano*

in the

Garrison Theatre, 1st and 2nd April, 1955

Conductor - - A. R. M. Mathewson
Accompanist - - Mrs J. Dalziel

Price — SIXPENCE

Iris Loveridge Programme.
(Courtesy of Shetland Archives)

Bride was very challenging. It was good to hear some songs from Norway, sung by Hilary Campbell, set to music by Mr Mathewson. Miss Loveridge stayed with Dr Constance Yule. She had been warned by Dr Yule that the house had young children and had replied replied: "I am not a temperamental pianist". Apart from those people we have already met, new names include Mr Alfred Harcus, technical teacher at the Anderson Institute, who was well known for a humorous act which involved sawing up a violin; Jack Scott, son of McGowan Scott; Douglas Smith, the environmental officer and son of Jennie Campbell; and Dr Constance Yule.

1955 Iris Loveridge concert. Back row: Mima Dalziel, Drew Robertson, Robbie Laurenson. A. W. Smith, Henry Hurlock, Jack Scott, Norman Brass, Mrs R. H. Neven-Spence, McCulloch or Phillipson. Front row: Geoffrey de Mercado, Beatrice Hunter, Erik Manson, Douglas Smith, T. M. Y. Manson, Hilary Campbell, A. R. M. Mathewson, Iris Loveridge, Jessie Leask, Dr Yule, Bertha Gray, Jack Goodlad, Alfie Harcus. *(Courtesy of Lerwick Orchestra)*

The reviews were quite good. The *News* stated: "Many people were under the spell of Friday's performance and could not resist the second concert on Saturday. The whole concert was a marked success largely due to the participating of two outstanding musicians, round whom the concert was built, Miss Iris Loveridge and Miss Hilary Campbell. The first part of this concert began with the well-known overture to the *Marriage of Figaro* by Mozart. Straight away there was a great improvement in the standard of the orchestra, an improvement which was to spread all over the concert. There was much life in that overture. A very grand pianist was Miss Loveridge but not a pianist only as everybody noticed at both concerts, she is also a great orchestral soloist helping with a simple

Mrs Hilary Harmer (née Campbell).
(Courtesy of Mrs Harmer)

glance the entry of the cellos or the clarinet or oboe, everything which makes the Schumann concerto movement more powerful and more enjoyable. It may be permissible to mention that the lack of bassoon handicapped it here. Miss Campbell appeared singing two songs set by the conductor Mr A.R.M. Mathewson who had also composed the second one. The first song was originally a violin melody composed by Ole Bull a Norwegian virtuoso with English words by Vagaland (Mr T.A. Robertson) based on the Norwegian words setting entitled *The Saeters Girl's Sunday*. The second Norwegian lullaby by Nordahlg Grieg translated into Shetlandic by Vagaland has been given a charming musical setting by Mr Mathewson. Miss Loveridge was naturally accorded a great ovation and in response she played with the utmost nerve Mendelssohn's *Rondo Capriccioso*. The concert ended with a very witty excerpt from Smetana's *The Bartered Bride*, the light-hearted trio by percussion trumpet and flute leading to the teasing duet and the riotous *Dance of the Comedians*."

As you can see in the programme, Beatrice Hunter was still in the orchestra, a veteran member since 1904.

Young players were now joining the senior members and Mr de Mercado was involved, along with Miss Spence, Father Ryan, George Abernethy, Mrs MacLaren and Masters MacLaren, Halcrow and Williamson. Dr T. M. Y. Manson assisted as conductor when necessary.

The 60s and 70s

Henry (Harry) Stevenson
Conductor 1968-1969

County music organiser, Mr Harry Stevenson conducted the orchestra with a view to accompanying the Choral Society for a performance of *The Creation*. This took place in May 1969. Three soloists from the south came to take part.

The review in *The Shetland Times* was an excellent one:

"Harry Stevenson is new music organiser for the county and from the moment he appeared on the rostrum, it became evident that a new and dynamic personality had appeared on the Lerwick musical scene. He was unquestionably in command of the whole assembly, and it was a pleasure to watch and listen to the way in which he controlled and guided all concerned."

Mr. Stevenson was a lively, enthusiastic conductor who always got what he wanted from the choir. He put all his energy into a performance. Apart from the work with the choir he played the organ for the "Big Kirk ", with some people finding it difficult to keep up with the speed he took the hymns.

Harry successfully organised large concerts, both with the choir and also the school children.

Mr James Halcrow
Conductor 1976-1983

In 1976, following a plea from Mr Tommy Sutherland, an advertisement was placed in *The Shetland Times* for interested parties to come forward and revive the orchestra. On 19th March a meeting was told that a good response had been achieved and Mr James Halcrow, B.Mus., M.A., was asked to be a conductor. This was not the first time that Mr Halcrow had worked with the Orchestra, for in 1961 Master James Halcrow was appointed accompanist following the resignation of Mrs J. Dalziel.

The Orchestra now consisted of: Roger Wildman, Michael Robertson, John Johnson, Lawrence Irvine, Vera Johnson, Michael Yielder,

LERWICK CHORAL SOCIETY

The
Creation

by Haydn

PATRICIA MACMAHON — SOPRANO
ROY BENSON — TENOR
JAMES KELMAN — BASS

— Conducted by —
HENRY STEVENSON

in the

Anderson Institute, Lerwick

on

TUESDAY, 27th MAY, 1969,
at 7.30 p.m.

ADMISSION BY PROGRAMME

Adults 5/- Juveniles 2/6

1969, The *Creation* programme.
(Courtesy of Vera Polson)

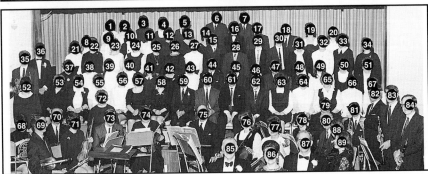

1969, *The Creation*. 1 Kathleen Gray, 2 Doris Moar, 3 Eileen Reid, 4 Wilma Halcrow, 5 Pat Laurenson, 6 Andrew Lambie, 7 James Blair, 8 A. Williamson, 9 S. Morrison, 10 R. Irvine, 11 R. C. S. Irvine, 12 Betty Anderson, 13 Ina Hunter, 14 Harriet Johnson, 15 ?, 16 Michael Peterson, 17 George Greig, 18 Lowrie Dalziel, 19 Nancy Greig, 20 Linda Cornes, 21 Janice Davidson, 22 Nell Jamieson, 23 Elizabeth Thomson, 24 Jeanie Hutchison, 25 Anne Rodger, 26 Nancy Conochie, 27 Claire Spence, 28 J. Gillespie, 29 Leslie Butler, 30 David Irving, 31 Lena Robertson, 32 Elizabeth Duthie, 33 Dorothy Bulter, 34 Eva Leask, 35 Harry Johnstone (visiting horn), 36 Harry Stevenson, 37 Lizzie J. Henry, 38 Drina Ramsay, 39 M. L. Leask, 40 W. T. Leask, 41 C. Hurlock, 42 M. R. Furnival, 43 Bella Hunter, 44 I. M. Furnival, 45 Ian McDill, 46 Alex Twatt, 47 Eddie Henry, 48 Marion Irvine, 49 Elizabeth Mullay, 50 Pryde Johnson, 51 J. Moncrieff, 52 Sheila Bruce, 53 Daisy Ratter, 54 Betty Stride, 55 Margaret Manson, 56 Kathleen Birnie, 57 Anne Gray, 58 Pat Cruickshank, 59 Alex Andrews, 60 Angus Laurenson, 61 Tom Ramsay, 62 C. G. Inman, 63 Jessie Forbes, 64 Barrie Hunter, 65 Chrissie Stevenson, 66 M. Tait, 67 Marion Young, 68 M. Webster (visiting horn), 69 J. Tyldesley, 70 Harold Stove, 71 Myra Banks (visiting violin), 72 Bertha Gray, 73 F. Bigwood, 74 Vera Johnson, 75 Jack Goodlad, 76 Merle Ingram, 77 Pam Smith, 78 E. Hollister (visiting oboe), 79 Drew Robertson, 80 T. M. Y. Manson, 81 George Johnson, 82 Billy Dalziel, 83 Tommy Sutherland, 84 R. Howie (visiting clarinet), 85 Roy Benson (tenor), 86 Patricia MacMahon (soprano), 87 James Kelman (bass), 88 Joanna Tyldesley, 89 A. E. Bowie (visiting flute). *(Courtesy of Pam Smith, © Dennis Coutts)*

John Goodlad and Bertha Gray on the violin.

Nancy Laurenson; Derek Henrikson playing viola; Mrs Pam Smith and Julie Smith with cello; Albert Rendall double bass; David Robertson, Barry Leith and Mortimer Manson with flute; Thomas Sutherland and Myra Ferguson clarinet; William Carter trumpet; Gilbert Irvine trombone; Drew Robertson and Douglas Johnstone percussion.

James Halcrow. *(Courtesy of Mrs A. Halcrow)*

The Orchestra continued to support the Choral Society and play at concerts within Church premises. Dr Manson continued to be secretary, Mr Douglas Johnstone and Mrs Pam Smith (both Maths teachers at the Anderson High School) were treasurer and chairman respectively. Mrs Pam Smith also founded the Shetland Youth Orchestra. Two music teachers with the education department were involved at this point, Richard and Lindsay Powell. Richard conducted the orchestra for a brief spell and Lindsay, a flute teacher, organised a large successful wind band.

Mike Blyth
Conductor 1983-1988

Mr Mike Blyth took over the conductorship of the Lerwick Orchestral Society after the committee advertised jointly with the Choir for conductors. Mr George Baker became choirmaster.

Mike came to Shetland in 1976 from Fife to work as a class music teacher. His main instruments are double bass, French horn and bagpipes.

The wind section became quite large under Mike and some players remain members today. There was, and still is, a shortage of violin players. Support was given to the Choral Society at concerts but it was Mike who allowed the orchestra to regain its independence and perform concerts by itself. The Brass Band helped in this respect as did the Junior Orchestra.

The leader at this time was Mr Roger Wildman, an accomplished musician and teacher in the school. Others members at the time included Mrs Pam Smith, founder of the junior orchestra, Mrs Bertha Gray, a player who had been with the orchestra back in the 1940s, Rev. David Monkton, John Shepherd, Mr Douglas Johnstone, Mr and Mrs Harold Exton, Rita Perkins (with her dog Felicity), Richard Edwards, Helen Kirkwood, Helen Dickson, Christine

Heather Oswald, Mike Blyth, Richard Edwards, Pam Smith, John Shepherd, David Monkton and Mortimer Manson. *(Courtesy of John Shepherd)*

Todd, Alan Gifford, Heather Butler, Rhonda Carryer, Merle Ingram, Brian Hill, Shona Owen, Susan Cooper, Fiona Baker, Kate and Caroline Dilloway and Heather Oswold. Mrs Lindsay Powell, and her youth wind band, also joined the adults.

Over the years the orchestra has collaborated with Islesburgh Drama Group. Productions include *South Pacific* in 1987. This involved a small section of the orchestra with Liz Kerr as musical director.

Enid Belshaw
Conductor 1988-1993

Miss Belshaw, a professional musician, came to Shetland from the North Cheshire College where she held the post of senior lecturer in Music Studies. Her subject was harmony and her instrument the piano. Miss Belshaw has chosen Shetland as her retirement home, and lives in an old church which has been converted into

Miss Belshaw.

Practice night at the Anderson High School. *(Courtesy of Nigel Martin)*

1987, *South Pacific.* *(Courtesy of Vera Polson)*

George Baker conducting at the Town Hall in December, 1985. Orchestra members are: 1 Rev David Monkton, 2 Bernadette Porter, 3 Marie Seery, 4 Teresa Morland, 5 Gordon Yeaman, 6 Elaine Sharwood, 7 Rodger Wildman, 8 Heather Oswald, 9 Bertha Gray, 10 Mrs Kate Dilloway, 11 T. M. Y. Manson, 12 Rita Perkins, 13 Heather Bulter, 14 Martin Radford, 15 Rohonda Carryer, 16 Mike Blyth, 17 Kay Laidlaw, 18 Elizabeth Monkton, 19 Caroline Dilloway, 20 Shona Watt, 21 Sylvia Halcrow, 22 Richard Edwards, 23 Susan Cooper.   *(Courtesy of Pryde Johnson)*

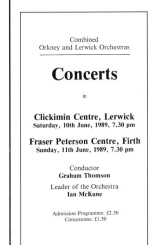

Combined
Orkney and Lerwick Orchestras

Concerts

in

Clickimin Centre, Lerwick
Saturday, 10th June, 1989, 7.30 pm

Fraser Peterson Centre, Firth
Sunday, 11th June, 1989, 7.30 pm

Conductor
Graham Thomson

Leader of the Orchestra
Ian McKune

Admission Programme: £2.50
Concessions: £1.50

Lerwick Orchestra
and
St Ola Singers

CONCERT

in

Lerwick Town Hall

Wednesday, 26th April, 1989

at 7.30 pm

Conductor: Enid Belshaw
Leader of the Orchestra: Maria Seery
Vocal Soloists: Nigel Morries, Bass
Josephine MacRae, Soprano
Christine Morries, Contralto
Flute Soloist: Brian Hill

Admission Programme: £2
Concessions: £1

Shetland's First
Promenade Concert
Clickimin Centre,
Saturday, 26th August, 1989, 7.30 pm
Compère: ALAN INKSTER

● PROGRAMME ●

Lerwick Orchestra:
Farandole from L'Arlesienne — Suite No. 2 ....Bizet
Four Waltzes ....Schubert
The Clog Dance from "La Fille mal Gardée" ....F. Herold
Dance of the Tumblers from the Snow Maiden ......Rimsky-Korsakoff

Lerwick Choral Society:
"How Lovely are Thy Dwellings" from The Requiem ....Brahms
Ca' The Yowes (Arr. W. Gilmour)

Lerwick Brass Band:
Music for the Royal Fireworks ....G. F. Handel
Selection: "The Pirate of Penzance" ....Sullivan

INTERVAL

Choral Society:
The Sound of Music ....Rodgers and Hammerstein
Moon River ....H. Mancini

Brass Band:
Indian Summer ....Eric Ball
Finlandia ....Sibelius

Orchestra:
Radetzky March ....J. Strauss
Pomp and Circumstance — March No. 1 in D ....Ed. Elgar
Jerusalem ....Parry
(Arr. W. Gilmour)

Three concert programmes from 1989. Promenade, Orchestra with St Ola Singers and Combined Orkney and Lerwick Orchestras. *(Courtesy of Enid Belshaw and author)*

a dwelling house and a small concert hall. The Orchestra had a run of very successful concerts in 1989 with the Brass Band, Choral Society and St. Ola Singers, which were well attended. The leader at this time was Jill Ford also joined by Dennis Shepherd, Rebecca Morritz, Maria Seery, Georgie Grant and Donald Stout. During that year there was a visit from the Orkney Orchestra, who combined forces with the Lerwick Orchestra for two performances, one in Brae, and one in the Clickimin Centre. Miss Belshaw organises the small singing group called the St Ola Singers from her The Old Kirk.

Dr. T. M. Y. Manson and the present day

Dr Thomas Mortimer Yule Manson, M.A., LL.D.
Treasurer 1937-1947
Secretary 1947-1989

A notable event in 1989 was the retirement as secretary of Dr Manson. Mortimer Manson, born in 1904 (and named after the doctor who delivered him), was the youngest son of Thomas Manson, the first conductor of the Lerwick Amateur Orchestral Society. Dr Manson's admirable record of service reads 10 years as treasurer and 42 years as secretary. Up until his retirement he was as busy as ever organising three concerts during 1989.

His instrument was the flute. He had been given one for his 14th birthday only to find it was of a different key from the rest of the Boys' Brigade. He had

The Boys' Brigade Flute Band, with T. M. Y. Manson leading, on the Lower Hillhead in 1944. Front row (left to right): Oliver Pottinger, Jim Spence and Douglas Smith.   *(Courtesy of Shetland Museum)*

to spend all the Christmas holiday practising to enable the flute to be the same as the other players.

Mortimer entered the printing works with his father on his return from Edinburgh University, where he had graduated M.A. in English and History in 1929. He had not played his flute at Varsity but concentrated upon it on his return, being very involved with the Boys' Brigade from 1939-1946 and Brass Band conductor from 1959-1964.

In 1951 Dr Manson was presented with the degree of Doctor of Laws by Aberdeen University for the enormous amount of work he put into organising the First Viking Congress. It was the British Council in Aberdeen who first contacted Mortimer to draw up a syllabus for the congress. As well as all the details of the congress, Mortimer arranged the social side, and this enabled him to involve the Orchestra.

The Shetland News closed down in 1963. Most people might have retired at this stage but not Dr Manson. He seemed as busy as ever, involved in The Shetland Movement, the Shetland Folk Society, the restoration of Arthur Anderson's birth place at the Böd of Gremista and becoming a member of Shetland Islands Council at the age of 78. He served eight years as a councillor,

The Brass Band in 1960 with T. M. Y. Manson conductor.
(Courtesy of Mrs H. Gould and the Brass Band)

only giving up on account of age and impaired hearing. The organisational skills needed to put on concerts is enormous. The Promenade Concert in 1989 took a lot of work. Dr. Manson undertook it all, never failing the orchestra in any way.

Dr Manson has been a great source of encouragement to the present secretary, and is the inspiration behind this booklet.

Neil Morris
Conductor 1993 to the present day

After a concert in St Columba's Church in December 1992 the Annual General Meeting at The Old Kirk in Whiteness on 19th January elected Mr Neil Morris as their conductor. Practice re-commenced at Isleburgh Community

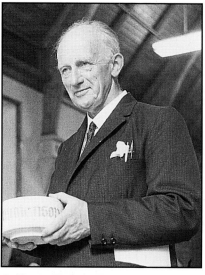

Dr Thomas Mortimer Yule Manson receiving a bowl presented to him at the 1969 Historical Congress in the Town Hall.
(Courtesy of Mr Robert Crawford)

Centre each Tuesday. At the beginning the turnout was small and it looked as if we would never get an orchestra together. Neil Morris, an excellent flute player, and woodwind teacher for the schools, spent time writing out parts to suit the available members. You might remember that it was in 1952 that the orchestra minuted that success had been due to Mr Ronnie Mathewson scoring the music for the available players, and that they asked him to do the

LERWICK ORCHESTRAL SOCIETY

CHRISTMAS CAROL CONCERT

on Monday 13th December 1993
in St Columbus Church

Concert in aid of the Macmillan Nurse Appeal

PROGRAMME:

CAROL: 'O Come All Ye Faithful'
Francis Chagrin - Renaissance Suite
CAROL: 'Still The Night'
Raymond Parfrey - Three Tunes
CAROL: 'As With Gladness Men of Old'
de Boismortier - Concerto
CAROL: 'Hark! The Herald-Angels Sing'
Two Pieces for Flute & Piano from the 'Snowman' - Howard Blake
CAROL: 'The First Nowell'

Lerwick Choral Society

Christmas
Concert

with the Lerwick Orchestra
in the Town Hall
on Tuesday 6th December
& Wednesday 7th December 1994
at 7:30pm

Conducted by
Bob Heaton
Accompanist
Christina Montgomery

Lerwick Orchestra

Spring Concert

at
Lerwick Town Hall

on
Wednesday 11th May 1994
7:30 pm

Three programmes from concerts by Neil Morris. *(Courtesy of author and Choral Society)*

same again, which he reluctantly agreed to do. This takes a great deal of time but, as in 1952, it seems to be the best solution for a small group of amateur players like ours.

A small concert in St Columba's Church in 1993 was well received. While a little short of repertoire (the orchestra offered to play the concert again as we seemed to finish very early!) we had got back into the way of practising regularly and giving concerts.

In May 1994 we took ourselves to the Town Hall and enjoyed performing the *Symphony No 29* in A major by Mozart. (We also made a small profit!)

Our next two concerts were with the Choral Society in the Town Hall and were well received. These consisted of a Christmas concert in 1994 conducted by Bob Heaton, and *The Creation* by Haydn (or Hadyn as printed on the programmes!) in May of 1995 conducted by Neil.

The 1996 orchestra is;

Patron — John Scott

Violin — Mhairi Mackinnon (Leader)

              Eunice Groat

              Theresa Moreland

1995 Town Hall with the Choral Society. *The Creation*. Back row: Brian Hill, Rebecca Moritz, Bob Heaton, Christina Montgomery. Second row: Marcia Galvin, Morven Mackinnon, Nigel Hallet, Elizabeth Robinson, Graham Anderson, Phillip Eost, Anna Stout, Malcolm Ferguson. Seated: Hilary Musgrave, Karen Griffiths, Mhairi MacKinnon, Neil Morris, Susan Cooper, Jenny Woods.
(Courtesy of Mr John Coutts)

Violin — David Henry
Viola — Bob Heaton (Chairman)
 Gwen Exton
Cello — Sarah McPherson
 Anna Purdy
 Kathryn Dray
Bass — Shona Owen
Flute — Christina Montgomery (Committee Member)
 Brian Hill (Treasurer)
 Rebecca Moritz (Refreshment Organiser!)
 Elizabeth Robinson (Librarian)
Clarinet — Philip Eost
 Marcia Galvin
 Susan Cooper (Secretary)
Saxophone — Katy Jenkins
 Barbara Lines
Horn — Harold Exton
Basson — Malcolm Ferguson
 Morven Mackinnon

We now have financial assistance from the Shetland Arts Trust for which we are very grateful.

In the 1950s a member of the orchestra was told by a Shetland lady that she would not be paying good money to come and listen to "High class musical dirt!" Let's hope the public of today don't support that view. We need players, we need an audience and let us hope we are not too high class. Come and join us.

Members' Music

People connected with the orchestra over the last 95 years have composed and arranged music, both classical and folk.

Some are well known and popular today, such as the Up-Helly-A' Song; music by Thomas Manson; *The Norseman's Home* arranged by Ronnie Mathewson and *Rowin Foula Doon*, music by T.M.Y. Manson.

Other compositions are not so well known, so it might be interesting to include a selection to give an all-round picture of the achievements of nearly 100 years making music with the Lerwick Orchestral Society.

Words by George Stewart, melody by Thomas Manson. *(Courtesy of Shetland Library)*

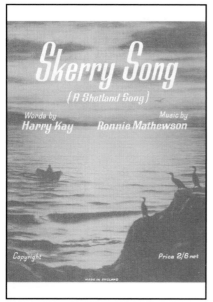

Cover design by Billy Kay

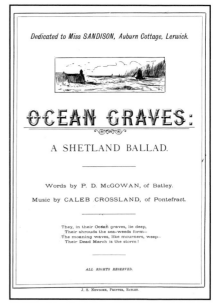

(Courtesy of Shetland Library)

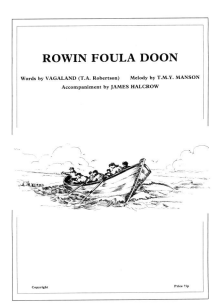

ROWIN FOULA DOON

Words by VAGALAND (T.A. Robertson)   Melody by T.M.Y. MANSON
Accompaniment by JAMES HALCROW

Copyright   Price 75p

Composed by Thomas Manson.
(Courtesy Shetland Library)

Melody by T. M. Y. Manson.
(Author's own copy)

Words by L. J. Nicolson   **Shetland Lullaby.**   Melody by W. Yorston.
Accompaniment by Thos. Manson.

Softly, softly humin grey
Ower da sea is creepin',
An' it's nedder nicht nor day,
Wakin' time, nor sleepin';
But da waves upo' da shore
Whisper still my lammie,
Doun da lum, an' troo da door;
Cuddle close to mammie.
Cosier du couldna be—
Hert o' my hert, life o' me.

Bonnie blue een blinkin' fast,
Peerie mootie lammie;
Sleep has ta'en de noo at last,
Cuddlin' close to mammie.
Blissens be attendin' de,
Happy be dy wakin',
For wir ain comes fae da sea,
Whin da day is breakin'.
Daybreak, licht o' hame is he—
Hert o' my hert, life o' me.

Accompaniment Thomas Manson.

53

Bibliography

The Shetland Violinist: The Gideon Stove Tune Book. Ed. Magnus J. Stove.

Lerwick During The Last Half Century, 1867-1917. Thomas Manson.

"Music in Shetland" by Ronald Popperwell, in *Essays in Shetland History*, ed. Barbara Crawford.

Reid Tait scrapbooks in Shetland Archives.

A Lerwick Miscellany. E. S. Reid Tait.

The Giving Years. James Irvine.

Sons and Daughters of Shetland. Margaret S. Robertson.

Manson's Shetland Almanac and Advertiser.

Night Scented Stock in Bloom? Martha Robertson.

Shetland Folk Book Vol IX. Ed. John Graham and Brian Smith

Northern Isles Connections. Ed. Barbara E. Crawford.

Da Sangs at a'll Sing Ta Dee. Ed. T. A. Robertson 1973.

Da Street. Aurora YESC

The Shetland Sketch Book. W. F. Clark

Illustrations

CHAPTER ONE; The early years
1904 group.
Advert 1904 concert.
1904 concert programme.
Thomas Manson.
1907 letter of engagement.
Manson family tree.
Gideon Stove.
A tea party.
Louisa Leisk.
Beatrice Hunter.
Brass Band.
Dutchies, Up-Helly-A'.
Bob McKay.
Abernethy Shop.
1906 Orchestra.
Magnus Sutherland.
1910 programme.

CHAPTER TWO; The Gilbert and Sullivan Operas
G & S Nucleus of orchestra members.
Mrs A. J. Smith.
Erik Manson.
Alex Linklater.
Patience 1926.

CHAPTER THREE; A.R.M.Mathewson
1939 Programme and tickets.
Alger Family.
Jack Goodlad.
Mrs George Gray.
Mrs Sidney Leask.
The New Players.
R.M.Y. Johnson.
Ronald G. Popperwell.
G.I. de Mercado.

CHAPTER FOUR; Post War
Miss Jean P. Boyd.
Messiah Programme.

Messiah 1947.
Harold Stove.
D.K. Gilbertson.
Mr & Mrs A.W. Smith.
Joe Linklater.
1951 Orchestral concert programme.
Helly Hoy 1952.
Helly Hoy programme.
1955 concert programme.
Iris Loveridge with Orchestra.
Mrs H. Harmer.

CHAPTER FIVE; The 60s and 70s
The Creation programme.
The Creation 1969.
James Halcrow.
Social evening.
Miss E. Belshaw.
Practice night at the high school.
South Pacific 1987.
George Baker at the Town Hall, 1995
Three concert programmes, 1989.

CHAPTER SIX; Dr T.M.Y.Manson & the Present Day
Flute Band.
Brass Band.
Dr Manson.
Three concert programmes.
Town Hall concert, 1995.

CHAPTER SEVEN; Members Music
Front sheet music.
a/ The Tooin 'o' wir Boat
b/ Skerry Song
c/ Da Last Noost
d/ Running Free
e/ Ocean Graves
f/ Te Deum Laudamus
g/ Rowin Foula Doon
h/ Shetland Lullaby